BIRDS
OF THE
AMERICAS
COLORING BOOK

IDENTIFIER GUIDE

BIRDS
OF THE
AMERICAS
COLORING BOOK

IDENTIFIER GUIDE

amber
BOOKS

ISBN: 978-1-78274-508-2

Published by
Amber Books Ltd
74–77 White Lion Street
London
N1 9PF
United Kingdom
www.amberbooks.co.uk
Appstore: itunes.com/apps/amberbooksltd
Facebook: www.facebook.com/amberbooks
Twitter: @amberbooks

Project Editor: Sarah Uttridge
Design: Mark Batley
Picture Research: Terry Forshaw
Illustrations: JB Illustrations

Manufactured in China

1 4 6 8 10 9 7 5 3 2

American Robin
Turdus migratorius

Contents

Red-cockaded Woodpecker
Leuconotopicus borealis

Wood Duck

There are many people who consider these colourful American swamp ducks to be one of the most beautiful of all species of waterfowl.

Northern Pintail

With their slimline bodies, elongated tails and skilful aerial acrobatics, the elegant Northern Pintail is often referred to as 'the greyhound of the air'.

SN 5/29/17

Northern Shoveller

Shovellers are also known as
Spoonbill Ducks because of their
unique bills, which are large and
shaped like a spatula.

Mallard

With their waddling walk and their renowned quacking call, Mallards are probably the best known and distinctively duck-like of all duck species.

Snow Goose

The large, white Snow Goose has two subspecies, which differ from each other in size, and breeds in the high Arctic.

Greater Scaup

Greater Scaups are a gregarious species. They are most often seen across northern sea coasts where they breed, gathering in marshes and brackish, saltwater bogs.

Brent Goose

The Brent Goose breeds in the high Arctic. There are two distinct species; These can be distinguished by the colour of the breast.

Canada Goose

The widespread Canada Goose is as celebrated for its evocative honk and yodelling as it is for its distinctive black and white plumage.

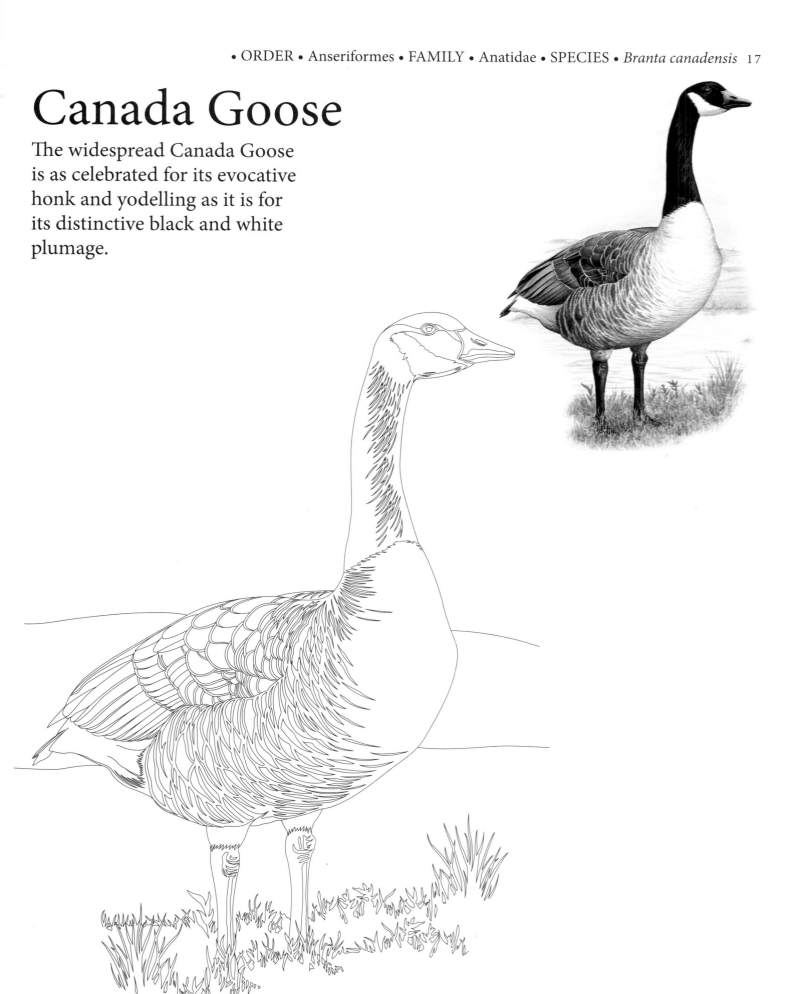

Hawaiian Goose

This goose is the official bird of the
US state of Hawaii, and is known
locally as the Nene.

Mute Swan

With its exquisite beauty and form,
it is easy to see why Ancient Britons
regarded Mute Swans as sacred.

Harlequin Duck

This duck is known by almost a dozen different names, but is most often called Lords and Ladies in North America and Harlequin Duck in Europe.

Goosander

Goosanders are expert hunters – and they need to be. Goosander chicks require around 33kg (72lb) of fish to fuel their change into adults.

Common Eider

The soft, warm breast feathers of
the female Eider have long been
used to fill quilts. They are also
useful for keeping the Eider warm
in its harsh living environment.

Ruby-throated Hummingbird

The tiny Ruby-throated
Hummingbird is no larger than a
ping-pong ball, but beats its wings
80 times a second when flying.

Little Auk

They may be no bigger than Starlings, but Little Auks are a hardy breed. They make their homes in the ice-laden seas of the North Atlantic.

Puffin

Don't be fooled by these brightly coloured clowns of the sea. Despite their comical appearance, these extraordinary seabirds are agile, skilled hunters.

Common Guillemot

Guillemots are so numerous
that, in their breeding colonies
(loomeries), as many as 20 birds
may occupy just 1 sq m
(10.75 sq ft).

Little Ringed Plover

The tiny and speedy Little Ringed Plover breeds near lakes, streams and also in man-made structures such as gravel pits.

Semipalmated Plover

The plump-breasted Semipalmated
Plover, a shore bird, can be found
along coasts and river estuaries.

Grey Plover

The Grey Plover is a strongly migratory bird, and can be found in coastal areas almost all over the world.

Piping Plover
Charadrius melodus

Herring Gull

For many of us, the raucous cry of
the Herring Gull will forever be
associated with lazy summer days
spent at the seaside.

Common Gull

The Common Gull breeds along coastlines and large lakes, often in big noisy colonies.

Black-legged Kittiwake

The Kittiwakes are the only type of
gull that nest exclusively on cliffs
and rocky ledges.

Ruddy Turnstone

The small, agile Ruddy Turnstone is a familiar wading bird seen along coastlines almost all over the world.

Sanderling

The Sanderling, a type of Sandpiper, is a small wading bird that can be seen running endlessly back and forth across the sand to escape the waves.

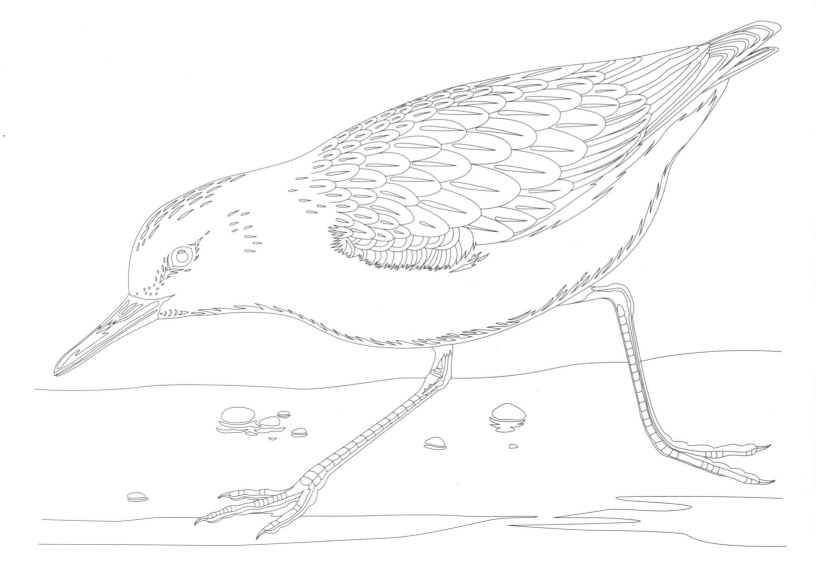

Dunlin

Dashing up and down the seashore
like little, pot-bellied, wind-up
toys, Dunlin are one of the most
popular of all waders.

Red Knot

The Red Knot is often seen in flocks; and during migrations these may number tens of thousands of birds.

Purple Sandpiper

The Purple Sandpiper often breeds
in barren, inhospitable places, and
has to fly to the coast to feed.

Common Snipe

It is the Common Snipe's zig-zagging flight that makes it so popular with hunters. In fact, especially skilled shots are known as snipers.

Whimbrel

Although Whimbrels are always a joy to watch, it is their plaintive cries that make them one of the most memorable of all wading birds.

Red-necked Phalarope

This species of Phalarope is one of
the easiest to identify – simply look
for the red neck that gives these
birds their common name.

Great Skua

This large, powerful bird is a real
pirate, often bullying other seabirds
to surrender their catch.

Green Kingfisher
Chloroceryle americana

Black Tern

With their streamlined, jet-black bodies, slate-grey wings and sharp, glossy bills, Black Terns make a handsome addition to the widespread Tern Family.

Arctic Tern

Arctic Terns are real avian athletes.
They regularly fly from pole to
pole to enjoy the benefits of two
summers a year.

Royal Tern

Royal Terns make their nests on
the ground of low-lying islands.
They defecate on the nest rim,
which eventually hardens and
reinforces the nest against flooding.

Great White Egret

The snowy Great White Egret will wait patiently for hours at a time by the water's edge for a tasty meal to pass by.

Cattle Egret

The Cattle Egret was originally found in southern Europe, but within the last century it has spread to most of the world.

Feral Pigeon

The Feral Pigeon is a familiar sight to all who live in larger cities, and is a descendant of the wild Rock Pigeon.

Golden Eagle

There are few birds in the world that can compare with the Golden Eagle in terms of majesty, beauty and sheer physical power.

Buzzard

The Buzzard, a large bird of prey,
is still a common sight in much
of Europe, probably because
it can live in a wide variety of
environments.

Hen Harrier

In the past, the extraordinarily elegant Hen Harrier was persecuted by landowners for poaching their game. Luckily, they are now protected in much of their range.

Bald Eagle

It seems fitting that the Bald Eagle, the national symbol of the USA, should be one of the great superpowers of the bird world.

Purple Finch
Carpodacus purpureus

California Condor

The majestic California Condor was once revered by ancient peoples. Now, sadly, its main claim to fame is that it is one of the world's rarest birds.

Northern Crested Caracara

Caracaras may be birds of prey but will also scavenge and steal from other birds, rather than hunt for themselves.

Merlin

The compact Merlin is justly famous for its beauty and hunting prowess. For many birdwatchers, just one glimpse of these graceful birds is truly magical.

Peregrine Falcon

Reaching speeds of over 290km/h (180mph), a Peregrine in a hunting dive is one of the fastest creatures on Earth.

Whooping Crane
Grus americana

Osprey

The unique and specialized Osprey is also known as the Sea Hawk, Fish Hawk or Fish Eagle, names that celebrate the birds' superb fishing skills.

Chicken

The chicken has been part of human history since our ancestors first learnt to farm, arriving in Europe around the seventh century BCE.

Grey Partridge

The Grey Partridge has declined dramatically throughout much of its European range because humans have cultivated much of its natural habitat.

Common Pheasant

The whirring flight and explosive
speed of the Common Pheasant
ensures that, for every bird shot,
some will always escape to boost
wild populations.

Rock Ptarmigan

This Rock Ptarmigan, an Arctic
bird, also breeds in mainland
Europe in high mountainous areas
above the tree limit.

Greater Prairie Chicken

With their elaborate mating dances and dramatic display plumage, the rare and beautiful Prairie Chicken could not be more different from its domestic counterpart.

American Goldfinch
Carduelis tristis

Great Northern Diver

In North America, Great Northern Divers are known as Loons because of the haunting, yodelling calls these birds make during the breeding season.

Shore Lark

The hardy Shore Lark makes its home in some of the bleakest locations, flourishing among Arctic tundra and barren, high mountains.

Bohemian Waxwing

Waxwings are named after their bright red wing tips, which are said to look like drops of freshly melted wax running down their feathers.

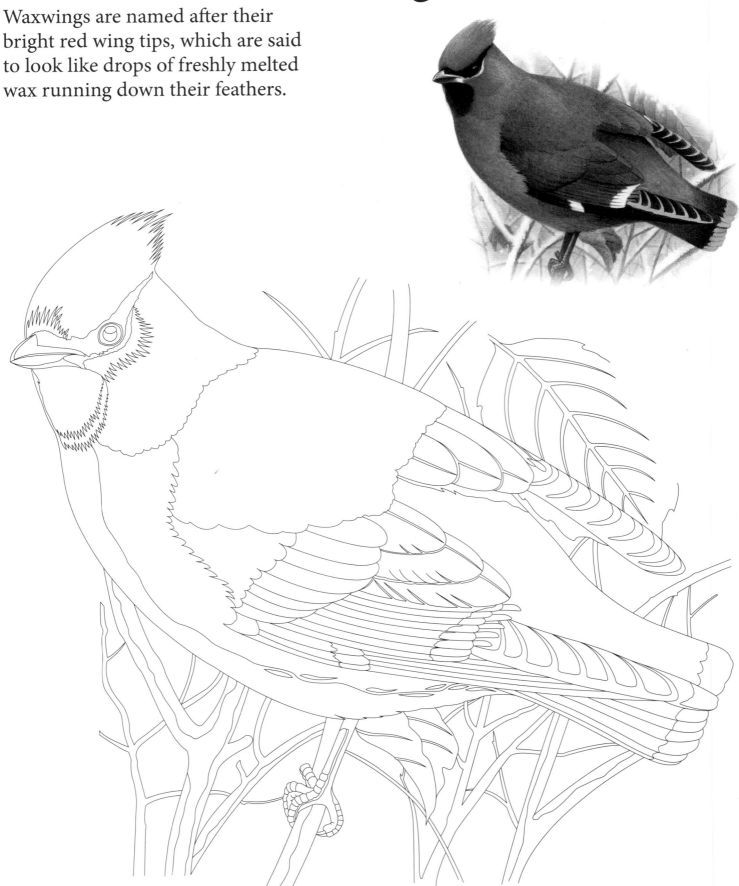

Florida Scrub Jay

Scrub Jays are one of the bird world's most sociable species, living in communal family groups that work together to help the breeding pair.

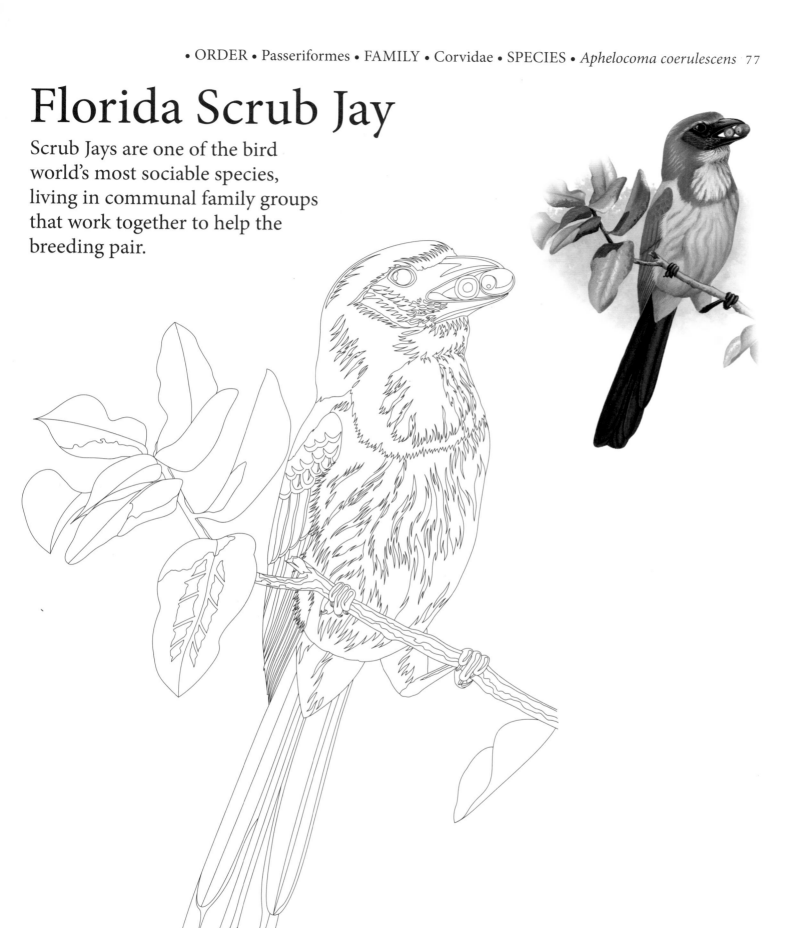

Raven

The Raven has an all-black plumage and a habit of feeding on corpses, so it is no wonder that some associate this bird with death and misfortune.

Blue Jay

The Blue Jay is a member of the
Crow Family, and is not closely
related to other Jays.

Magpie

Magpies are intelligent, sociable birds. Thanks to their dramatic black and white plumage, they are also one of the easiest to identify.

Evening Grosbeak

The Evening Grosbeak gets its common name from the loud chirruping calls that it is said to sing only as the sun begins to set.

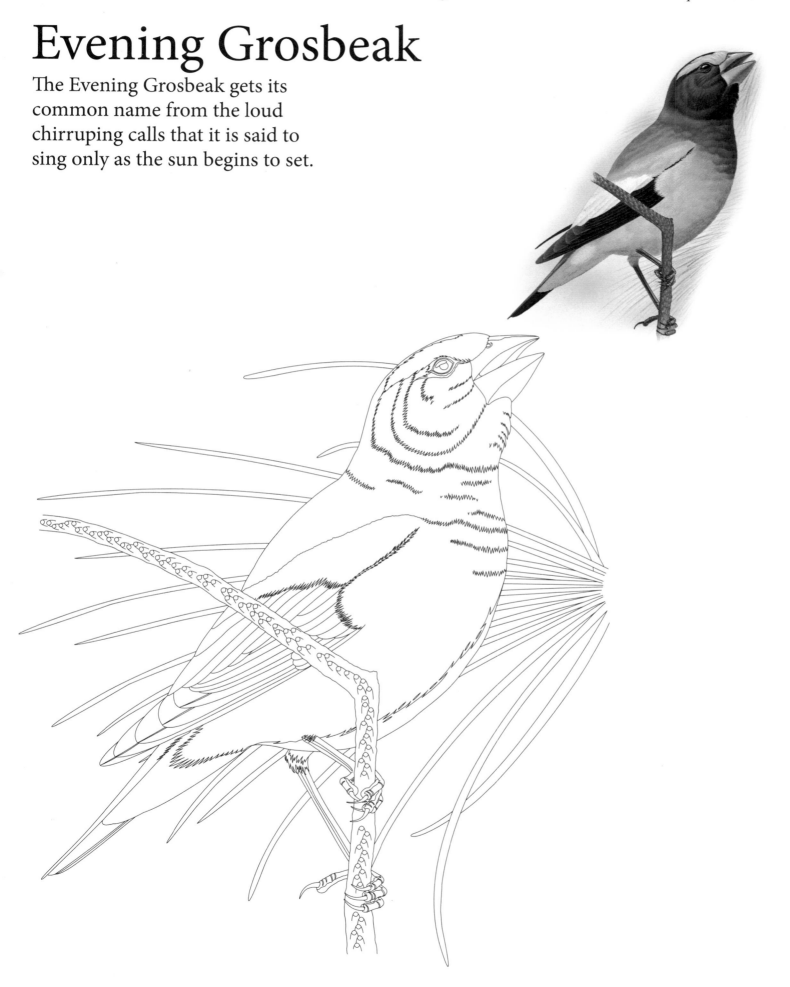

Common Crossbill

The Common Crossbill is aptly named, and is perfectly adapted for survival in conifer forests on a diet that would be impossible for most other birds.

Swallow

The fast-flying Swallow is familiar to most people in Europe and North America, and is often heralded as the harbinger of summer.

Sand Martin

The small Sand Martin arrives at its breeding grounds earlier than other Swallows, feeding on the insects of early spring.

Tree Swallow

Tree Swallows are graceful in the air but on the ground, whether they are fighting for territory or a mate, they are quarrelsome and aggressive.

Great Grey Shrike

Shrike are commonly known as Butcher Birds, thanks to their gruesome habit of impaling the bodies of their victims on thorn bushes.

Yellow Wagtail

True to the name, the familiar
Yellow Wagtail often bobs its long
tail up and down when searching
for food on the ground.

Northern Wheatear

The perky Northern Wheatear is
one of the easier moorland birds to
spot, thanks to its habit of perching
on a rock to announce its presence.

Yellow-rumped Warbler

With bright rumps and vivid
patches of yellow on their wings,
Yellow-rumped Warblers are one
of the easiest species of American
Warblers to identify.

Common Yellowthroat

With its bandit's mask and vibrant, yellow throat, the Common Yellowthroat is one of the most recognizable of all North American warblers. Only the male sings.

Rock Wren

The Rock Wren, a popular little bird, is one of the few Wrens to live up to its Latin Family name *Troglodytidae*, which means 'cave-dweller'.

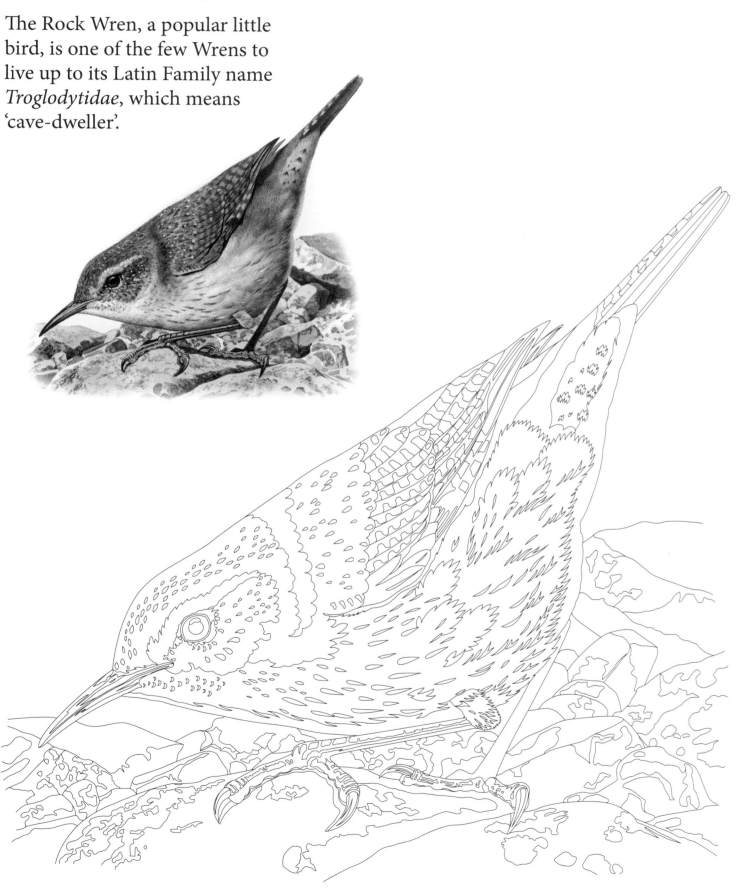

Winter Wren

Its tiny size, piercing song and
jaunty upturned tail make the
Winter Wren one of the easiest of
the small brown garden birds to
recognize. It also has the nickname
Jenny Wren.

Hermit Thrush

The Hermit Thrush is the smallest species of Thrush in North America, and is also considered to have the most beautiful song.

Golden-Cheeked Warbler
Dendroica chrysoparia

Eastern Kingbird

The Eastern Kingbird is a
Flycatcher, and despite the name is
actually found across most of
North America.

American Darter

American Darters are also known as Snakebirds. This is because when they swim only their neck appears above the water, and looks like a snake preparing to strike.

Magnificent Frigatebird

The Magnificent Frigatebird
is one of the bird world's most
accomplished fliers. In fact, it is so
skilled in the air that it can ride out
a hurricane.

Brown Pelican

In the case of the Brown Pelican,
the limerick boasting that 'his bill
can hold more than his belly can'
is really true.

Great Cormorant

In Norse legend, those who die at sea spend eternity on the isle of Utrøst, where they can visit loved ones disguised as the Cormorant.

Northern Gannet

Seabirds are rarely eaten, but the inhabitants of the Isle of Lewis, United Kingdom, consider the Gannet a delicacy. The taste is described as fish-flavoured chewing gum.

Greater Flamingo

With its bright pink plumage,
the Flamingo is a showy bird. Its
origins can be traced back four
million years.

Red-headed Woodpecker

The popular children's cartoon character Woody Woodpecker was modelled on the Red-headed Woodpecker.

Eurasian Three-toed Woodpecker

The Eurasian Three-toed Woodpecker
tends to be resident, although birds from
northern areas may fly south for the winter.

Northern Fulmar

The attractive Fulmar is best known for an ingenious, but unattractive habit. When danger strikes, it vomits oily gastric juices all over its attacker.

Great Shearwater

The Great Shearwater is a superb flier. It gets its name from the shearing motion it makes in the air as it moves sideways from air current to air current to save energy.

Manx Shearwater

The Manx Shearwater is a graceful
seabird that spends most of the
year fishing on the open oceans,
returning each spring to breed on
rocky islands.

Northern Cardinal
Cardinalis cardinalis

Short-tailed Shearwater

The Short-tailed Shearwater
migrates to its breeding grounds in
enormous flocks numbering tens of
thousands of individuals.

Tengmalm's Owl

Tengmalm's Owl takes its unusual
name from Peter Gustaf Tengmalm
(1754–1803), the Swedish naturalist
who first identified the species.

Short-eared Owl

The Short-eared Owl often emits
a series of deep 'po-po-po' sounds
while flying, but hunts
in complete silence.

Long-eared Owl

Unlike many other Owls, the
sizable, arresting-looking Long-
eared Owl often hunts in complete
darkness.

Burrowing Owl

Strange as it may seem, the small
Burrowing Owl spends most of
its life underground in specially
excavated burrows.

Snowy Owl

The voluminous and angelic
Snowy Owl is also known as the
Arctic Owl or Great White Owl,
and is well adapted for life in the
high north.

Great Horned Owl

The huge and commanding Great Horned Owl will even kill and consume other birds of prey.

Eastern Screech Owl

The tiny Eastern Screech Owl has piercing yellow eyes and prominent ear tufts. It is the most strictly nocturnal of all North American Owls.

Elf Owl

The Elf Owl may be no bigger than
a sparrow, but from its rounded
head to its hooked claws it is every
inch an Owl.

Barn Owl

With its pale face, dark eyes
and unearthly shrieks, the
Barn Owl is responsible
for its share of countryside
ghost stories.

Reddish Egret
Egretta rufescens

Birds Conservation Status

Wood Duck	Least Concern
Northern Pintail	Least Concern
Northern Shoveller	Least Concern
Mallard	Least Concern
Snow Goose	Least Concern
Greater Scaup	Least Concern
Brent Goose	Least Concern
Canada Goose	Least Concern
Hawaiian Goose	Vulnerable
Mute Swan	Least Concern
Harlequin Duck	Least Concern
Goosander	Least Concern
Common Eider	Near Threatened
Ruby-throated Hummingbird	Least Concern
Little Auk	Least Concern
Puffin	Vulnerable
Common Guillemot	Least Concern
Little Ringed Plover	Least Concern
Semipalmated Plover	Least Concern
Grey Plover	Least Concern
Herring Gull	Least Concern
Common Gull	Least Concern
Black-legged Kittiwake	Least Concern
Ruddy Turnstone	Least Concern
Sanderling	Least Concern
Dunlin	Least Concern
Red Knot	Near Threatened
Purple Sandpiper	Least Concern
Common Snipe	Least Concern
Whimbrel	Least Concern
Red-necked Phalarope	Least Concern
Great Skua	Least Concern
Black Tern	Least Concern
Arctic Tern	Least Concern
Royal Tern	Least Concern
Great White Egret	Least Concern
Cattle Egret	Least Concern
Feral Pigeon	Least Concern
Golden Eagle	Least Concern
Buzzard	Least Concern
Hen Harrier	Least Concern
Bald Eagle	Least Concern
California Condor	Critically Endangered
Northern Crested Carcara	Least Concern
Merlin	Least Concern
Peregrine Falcon	Least Concern
Osprey	Least Concern

Chicken	Least Concern
Grey Partridge	Least Concern
Common Pheasant	Least Concern
Rock Ptarmigan	Least Concern
Greater Prairie Chicken	Vulnerable
Great Northern Diver	Least Concern
Shore Lark	Least Concern
Bohemian Waxwing	Least Concern
Florida Scrub Jay	Vulnerable
Raven	Least Concern
Blue Jay	Least Concern
Magpie	Least Concern
Evening Grosbeak	Least Concern
Common Crossbill	Least Concern
Swallow	Least Concern
Sand Martin	Least Concern
Tree Swallow	Least Concern
Great Grey Shrike	Least Concern
Yellow Wagtail	Least Concern
Northern Wheatear	Least Concern
Yellow-rumped Warbler	Least Concern
Common Yellowthroat	Least Concern
Rock Wren	Least Concern
Winter Wren	Least Concern
Hermit Thrush	Least Concern
Eastern Kingbird	Least Concern
American Darter	Least Concern
Magnificent Frigatebird	Least Concern
Brown Pelican	Least Concern
Great Cormorant	Least Concern
Northern Gannet	Least Concern
Greater Flamingo	Least Concern
Red-headed Woodpecker	Near Threatened
Eurasian Three-toed Woodpecker	Least Concern
Northern Fulmar	Least Concern
Great Shearwater	Least Concern
Manx Shearwater	Least Concern
Short-tailed Shearwater	Least Concern
Tengmalm's Owl	Least Concern
Short-eared Owl	Least Concern
Long-eared Owl	Least Concern
Burrowing Owl	Least Concern
Snowy Owl	Least Concern
Great Horned Owl	Least Concern
Eastern Screech Owl	Least Concern
Elf Owl	Least Concern
Barn Owl	Least Concern

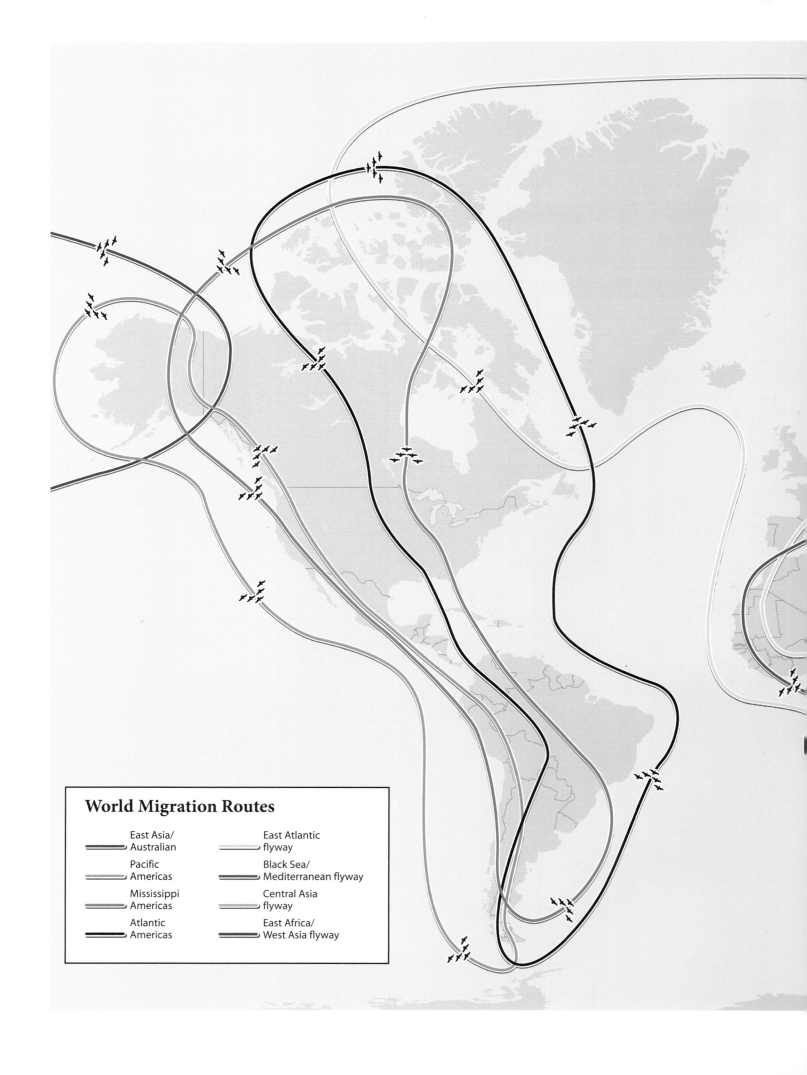

World Migration Routes

East Asia/ Australian		East Atlantic flyway	
Pacific Americas		Black Sea/ Mediterranean flyway	
Mississippi Americas		Central Asia flyway	
Atlantic Americas		East Africa/ West Asia flyway	

Broad-billed Hummingbird
Cynanthus latirostris